Learning Together

What Montessori can offer **your** family

By Kathi Hughes

Registered Charity No. 313636

About the author, Kathi Hughes

When I was growing up and did anything well, my mother would always say matter-of-factly, "That's because you're a Montessori kid." I attended Montessori schools from the age of two and a half to six, building my own foundation that has stuck with me throughout my life. I went on to train as a Montessori teacher at the Montessori Centre International in London and currently work from home as a distance learning tutor and proof-reader, but my main job is as a Montessori parent of three young children, Peter, Owen and Abigail, without whom I could not have written *Learning Together*.

Contents

'Effective parenting makes a proven difference to family life and unlocks a child's potential, but we know that it isn't easy! This book offers a balance of information for parents, giving uncomplicated explanations and guidance to increase understanding and knowledge and provides practical examples of how to nurture a child to reach their full potential.

The book addresses the fact that each child in every family is unique and will have differing needs, relating to parents with realistic practical examples of how to let a child learn at their own pace from everyday life in and around the home and outside of any nursery setting. In truth, things that parents may take for granted about bringing up their child provide opportunities to encourage natural development without the need for expensive toys, equipment, clubs and outings.

The information about brain and physical development relates well to the importance of allowing appropriate risk taking and behaviour management. It encourages any parent who has this knowledge to increase their child's independence and confidence which are the building blocks for school and adult life.

As a national body working with and supporting parenting organisations and practitioners, *Parenting UK* are pleased to be able to support the ethos of this new parenting book'.

parenting UK

Foreword

by Barbara Isaccs, Academic Director
Montessori Centre International

I was delighted when I was invited by the Montessori St. Nicholas charity to participate in this parenting project. True benefits of the Montessori approach for children can be seen when parents engage with Montessori's idea of "following the child" according to each child's unique potential.

It is the aim of the book to share with parents, what mothers, fathers and carers who know about the Montessori approach, have learned about their children and from Montessori – in other words, this is a book written by parents for parents. Whilst Montessori is renowned for its specialised learning materials it is not the purpose for this slender volume to instruct parents on how to use the specific Montessori apparatus. The book is about bringing some of the Montessori spirit into your home.

We hope that the many practical ideas and tips will be useful to everyone engaged with children in the home. They focus on understanding the child's unique development, organising the home appropriately and sharing in activities which will nurture independence, engagement, initiative and positive communication. This approach will support children's growing sense of self, of well-being and belonging.

Being a parent is a real challenge; getting to know one's children is another, accepting them for who they are rather than who we would like them to be is quite another. Everyone who comes across this book should be able to find some of the Montessori ideas useful as they bring new insights into your relationship with children and spark deeper understanding of ourselves and of our children.

Above all enjoy your children's company whilst reading a book, playing a game or doing a puzzle, running in the park or splashing in the sea – being together and learning from each other is the gift of parenting.

by Philip Bujak, Chief Executive
Montessori St Nicholas Charity

Learning to be a parent can be more challenging than any other part of our lives as adults and yet society does very little to prepare us for this vital journey. In the past, the family was a place where parenting skills could be learnt by observation of how our mum and dad did everyday things or how grandma and grandpa dealt with everyday problems. Indeed, that was perhaps the best way to learn. As the demands of family life continue to grow much of this learning by observation has disappeared. However over 100 years ago, Dr Maria Montessori based her life with children on scientific observation and her findings are as fresh and relevant today as they were then. These are captured here in this book and the title of *Learning Together* tells us that her key principle of child observing the adult and the adult observing the child is largely what good parenting is all about.

I pay a small tribute here to the vision of the trustees of the St Nicholas Charity. Their commitment and funding for better parenting initiatives enabled this book to be created. For the hundreds of thousands of new parents that are created each year I hope that those who find this book also find help in their own journey as they learn to become better parents.

Introduction

For the nine months before a baby is born, so much is focussed on pregnancy and the birth that it can almost come as a surprise to find that when it's over there is a brand new person in the house. In so many ways this new baby is all about potential. The young child is simply full of future possibilities. This is what makes being a mother or father so awe-inspiring; we can see the amazing powers that a new baby holds, even though she starts out completely dependent on us.

Starting from this perspective of the child's enormous potential, this book aims to take a fresh look at parenting. It is inspired by the ideas and writings of Maria Montessori, the founder of the Montessori approach to education. She believed that each child's potential held tremendous possibilities. Through extensive observation of children of all ages, she developed a philosophy of education that puts the child at its heart. This publication is designed to help you as a parent put your child at the heart of your home, and to unlock that amazing potential. *Learning Together: What Montessori can offer your family* aims to give you:

- a fuller understanding of the amazing potential of your child (Chapter 1)
- tools to unlock this potential (Chapter 2)
- concrete ideas you may want to try at home to nurture your child's potential (Chapter 3)
- ideas on how to prepare a child-friendly home to support independence (Chapter 4)

There are ideas to use with children of all ages, from newborn babies

" The young child is simply full of future possibilities."

through to toddlers and the older child as well. If you already have children you will probably find that you already do at least some of the things mentioned, if not many of them, because there is a lot of overlap between the ideas underlying a Montessori approach and parenting that respects the child as an individual.

Here in the UK, the first five years of life are referred to as the 'foundation years' and for good reason; these earliest experiences and interactions lay a foundation for future growth and development in every way. Montessori said that considering the amazing achievements and transformations the child goes through during the first three years of life, this stage could be considered "as long as a whole life". Current research on brain development is shedding more and more light on the importance of these earliest years, beginning at birth and even before, and parents are becoming increasingly aware of the potential this time holds for their child.

The baby's first smile, first steps, first word: all these amazing achievements are underpinned by the simple things the mother and

father do with their baby on a daily basis: talking, singing, holding, playing, and so on.

There has also recently been a lot of evidence showing us how important parenting and the home environment are as contributing factors in children's development. Bringing up children is probably the most challenging role any one of us will face in our lives, yet there is often little training for the job. No one manual will cover all the challenges we will face. What we hope to offer here is an approach that will help you develop trust and confidence in your own skills as parents, based on a deeper understanding of child development and the child's emerging needs. Developing a positive attitude towards your child based on freedom, respect and independence, combined with clear and simple boundaries, will help your child feel secure to explore and discover the possibilities and wonders of the wider world.

This is not meant to be a step-by-step guide to parenting, nor is it a 'how to' manual. There is a right way to be a parent, but it is your way. You know your child best.

A word about fathers

Fathers are no less important than mothers in helping their children develop. We say this explicitly because, historically, culturally and in research, fathers' impact has been overlooked and there has sometimes been an assumption that 'only mothers matter'. Further, many mothers and fathers believe that mothers have 'innate' skills with young children that fathers lack. In fact, men are no less naturally sensitive to babies' cues and needs than women are: it's a matter of familiarity and practice.

Chapter 1

The potential of the child

From the start the new baby's potential comes from his curiosity and natural drive to explore and make sense of the world around him. In the early months and years this natural curiosity is centred on developing an attachment to the baby's mother and father (and anyone else they see regularly such as brothers and sisters, or grandparents). Then, working outwards from this secure base, the baby begins to explore his surroundings through movement and his five senses, beginning with the way his own body moves and its potential, and then widening the perspective to explore the environment around him. Through all of this the new baby is driven by his need to become independent, to make his own mark on the world around him.

Bonding and brain development

In the first days and weeks after birth, the new baby is making a transition from life inside the womb to life in her new world. The goal is to make this transition as gradual and peaceful as possible. Interestingly, Montessori was ahead of her times in highlighting the importance of close physical contact with the mother immediately after birth. We now know that skin-on-skin contact with the father is very beneficial too – to both father and baby.

Human babies develop more out of the womb than any other animal,

> " Whenever we touch the child, we touch love. It is a difficult love to define; we all feel it, but no one can describe its roots, or evaluate the immense consequences which flow from it..."
>
> **Maria Montessori**
> *(The Absorbent Mind)*

Bonding and you

The gift of time

For me being a father is not about working ridiculous hours to earn the money to buy my daughter every latest gadget or fad. It was a bit of a revelation to me but I realised the greatest gift I could give her was time. Time to be 'present' and in her world, to slow down and just 'be' with her. To let her do things again and again without rushing her on. Being a dad is more than just being wheeled in for the 'rough and tumble' play but also for the long, cosy cuddles on her bed gazing up at the glow stars on her ceiling talking about our day. It feels like the bond we now have between us is a kind of stretchy band that will let her explore the world but still always feel connected.

Doug, father of two, ages 6 months and 3

On attachment

We adopted our wonderful daughter at 13 months. Apart from the usual delights and difficulties of parenting, there were other behavioural issues to consider, but the main goal was to give her a stable and loving home, allowing her the life opportunities all children deserve as they grow up. It was scary driving her back to our home after the week-long introduction at her foster carer's home, and initially she challenged interactions we had with her: feeding, changing, eye contact, not being comforted when hurt, and so on. But crucially, she'd developed a good attachment with her foster parent, with whom she had been placed from birth; although she obviously felt loss when leaving her, she had learnt how to attach and gradually, with patience, the resistance passed and it feels now as if we couldn't be closer.

It really has been a lovely journey from the start, although I think her sunny nature has made it easier (maybe her Dad would say that).

Anyway, it went so well, we found her a lovely little brother.

Patrick, father of two, ages 3 and 6

to allow them to adapt to their surroundings (which naturally vary greatly across the world). The brain is immature at birth, so in infancy it is still growing and connections or synapses are being made between different areas of the brain; the baby's brain more than doubles in weight in the first year of life. During this vital period of growth and development the baby is completely dependent on adults for survival as well as the all-important interaction, with others and with the environment, that will foster brain growth. Everyone and everything the baby comes into contact with contributes to his development.

In these early years the baby forms attachment bonds to her primary caregivers, usually the mother and father. Touch is vitally important at this stage, and 'wearing' the baby in a sling or carrier is a good way for both fathers and mothers to stay in close physical contact while also offering the baby the chance to take in what is around her (sounds, voices, smells, shades of light and dark). As the baby and her caregivers get to know one another, the caregivers respond by becoming more and more 'in tune' with the baby, responding to her needs and understanding the signals that the baby is happy, tired, hungry, anxious, and so on. The more one-on-one care a mother or father provides, the more 'in tune' he or she becomes with their baby: if one parent is always 'interpreting' the baby's needs to the other, then the less confident or available parent may

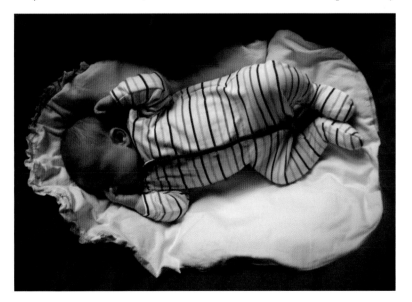

lag behind in learning. When parents provide this consistently available and present emotional base the baby begins to feel secure in her surroundings. The baby carries forward the impressions formed from this first relationship as an infant, and this is the foundation for further exploration and discovery.

Although as adults we do not consciously remember it, recent research has revealed the importance of consistent and connected caregiving in brain development in the early months and years. At birth the baby's brain handles basic functions only; it is still growing and changing and being shaped by these early social interactions. As different areas of the brain mature and develop, connections are made on neural pathways that will have a lifelong effect.

Babies rely on their caregivers to regulate stress for them because their still-developing brains mean that they can't yet do it themselves. How the baby learns to regulate his feelings in infancy has a key role to play in setting cortisol levels in the body, which has a life-long effect on how able a person is to cope with stressful situations.

So, how can the mother or father help a distressed baby? The first response is generally touch: picking up the baby, stroking him. Parents also naturally use a soothing voice, possibly singing a familiar calming song or simply

Rough-housing

Researchers are now beginning to appreciate the value of 'rough-housing' to children's development. Not only does sensitive and frequent rough-housing contribute to adult-child bonding but it has been associated with children's sense of security right through to adolescence. Rough-housing is so important and valuable that it should not be left only to dads: mothers can do it too, and if upper-body-strength holds you back as your child grows older, rough-housing by wrestling (letting the child win!) and rolling around on the floor can be wonderful.

saying "shh shh shh" in a rhythmic way. Babies respond to motion, so touch and a soothing voice are often accompanied by a rocking movement. Babies also naturally respond to facial expressions so these can be used to help a baby in distress calm down. Fathers and mothers tend to do all of this quite naturally. Parenting manuals will offer lots of differing opinions on how to respond to a crying baby but, as with so many decisions we make as parents, it's important to do what feels right for your baby, in any particular situation.

> Babies rely on their caregivers to regulate stress for them because their still-developing brains mean that they can't yet do it themselves."

> " Freedom of movement allows infants, and later toddlers and older children, to explore and learn about their world through sensory experiences."

The importance of movement

The first weeks of a baby's life are a time of amazing development. Although they may seem to 'do' very little they are in fact taking in huge amounts of information about the world around them and the people in it. Movement is the key to these first experiences of the world. Freedom of movement allows infants, and later toddlers and older children, to explore and learn about their world through sensory experiences.

In the beginning, newborns start out unable to hold their heads up, with random jerky movements of their arms and legs, but quite quickly within the first year the baby learns to control these movements. Newborns are also born with important reflexes or automatic movements that help them survive outside the womb.

Early days

Given complete freedom to move, say placed on a blanket on the floor, the baby will wave his arms and kick his legs. These early movements of kicking legs and waving arms may not look like much, but "(e)very time he kicks his legs and waves his arms he feels where his body begins and ends; when his foot hits the floor he starts to gain an inner sense of how long he is; when he reaches for an object he learns how much speed and force he needs to use to reach his target. More importantly he gradually learns where and when to slow down and stop the movement" (Sally Goddard-Blythe, *The Well-Balanced Child*).

The baby also begins by reaching out and touching things, then grasping things. When babies discover their own hands and feet they are fascinated by these amazing tools, and they gradually work out that they can do things with them, reaching out to bat at or kick a mobile, or grasping a toy and shaking it, banging it or putting it in their mouth to find out more about it.

Young babies benefit from both active and passive movement. For active movement, free time on the floor, unrestrained in any way, is perfect. However in the first weeks and months babies may well prefer to be held or carried, rather than being put down; your baby will let you know when she is ready and happy to begin exploring on her own. For passive movement, baby-wearing (carrying the baby on your body, in a

Reflexes

Some reflexes to look out for include:

- **the rooting reflex**, where the baby turns and opens his mouth to feed when his cheek is brushed
- **the Moro or startle reflex**, where if the baby's head and neck are unsupported her arms thrust outward
- **the palmar or grasp reflex**, where the baby will grasp a finger or other object when her palm is touched (you can take advantage of this to let older brothers or sisters 'hold hands' with a new baby)
- **the sucking reflex**, where the baby sucks to be fed; this is replaced by voluntary sucking around two months of age
- **the plantar or Babinski reflex**, where if you stroke the sole of the baby's foot his toes will spread out
- **the stepping or walking reflex**, where if you hold the baby on a flat surface she will move her feet as if taking steps
- **the tonic neck reflex**, where the baby assumes a 'fencing' position when lying on his back; with his head turned in one direction his arm and leg on that side will extend while the opposite arm and leg will bend so he appears to be fencing

sling or carrier) allows the baby to experience natural sensations of balance/movement from the adult carrying them, whereas time spent in car seats, buggies and infant seats limit opportunities to absorb natural rhythms of movement.

Crawling and walking

Babies naturally spend a lot of time lying on their backs, but time spent on the front ('tummy time') is important to build neck strength and the muscles in the arms, upper body and back while pushing up from the front. Interestingly time spent in a sling also builds strength in these core muscles as the baby holds himself against the adult and moves with them. Increasing control over movements and strength will soon lead to the baby rolling over, and before you know it moving along the floor towards a favourite toy (or the family cat, in our house). Crawling can take many forms; do not be surprised if your baby doesn't crawl in the traditional 'all-fours' manner. Some babies crawl for a long time before moving on to cruising (walking around holding on to furniture – coffee tables are great for this) and walking, while others skip out crawling and go straight to walking.

Into the second year

In the second year movement remains all-important as the child learns to walk with confidence and can access so much more of the world around him independently. This increasing independence will also be seen in new things such as drinking from a cup and having a go at getting dressed. Walking is only the beginning: new skills such as balancing, jumping, and running now become the focus.

As the infant moves through these stages of development it is important to give her enough time

The importance of children observing movement

Montessori believed (as do many) that children need to observe a movement (absorb it visually) before they can execute the movement themselves. Then the child can repeat the movement to master it. This is as important for a three year old as it is for a 2 month old.

For Caspar (3yrs) this means him observing me as I grip the pencil, as I hold a fork or a spoon. It is not enough to tell or instruct him what to do or how to do it. It is not enough to try and manipulate his little fingers around the pencil. He needs to see it and be around it. Not necessarily for me to give him a lesson but to ensure he has lots of opportunity during everyday life to see me write, to see me eat.

The same for Otis (2months), while he is at a very unique stage developmentally he needs to observe visually his own movements to gain an awareness of them before he can then reproduce or master them. For him this is looking at his hands as he moves them, opens and closes them or watching his own movements in the mirror with his aim being to master coordinated movement.

This is in part what Montessori meant when she wrote about children absorbing their environment. It is important that as parents we provide an environment that is enriched with lots of opportunity. By this I mean ensure your child has the opportunity to observe you in your every day life, and for the youngest of children give them the opportunity to observe themselves.

from Kylie D'Alton's blog How-We-Montessori

to fully develop each new skill and try not to move her on to the next thing too soon. If babies and children are regularly being pushed on to the 'next new thing' too soon and failing at it, they can start to feel discouraged. All babies will roll over/sit up/crawl/stand/walk when they are ready! Wait and watch, supporting the baby where she is *now*. Interestingly, you may often notice a disruption in your child's sleeping patterns, eating, energy levels, or moods just before a new skill suddenly emerges, often seemingly out of the blue.

"In development, the most important changes often start to take place before they can actually be seen, rather like seeds germinating beneath the ground. By the time a new developmental skill is evident, like seedlings emerging in the Spring, much of the organization, which is necessary for the skill to develop, has already taken place. The period of development that occurs 'in the dark' is as important as the practice of that new skill when it actually emerges."
Sally Goddard-Blythe (*The Well-Balanced Child*)

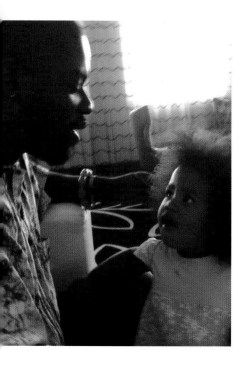

Communication

Alongside movement, the baby's amazing potential can be seen in her ability to communicate with others. This is true from the first days of life, when a baby's heart rate synchronizes with the heartbeat of a familiar caregiver when held. This may explain why an experienced parent or grandparent can often calm a baby down simply by holding him or her. This potential to communicate with others continues through to the early years, by which time the child has experienced tremendous developments in spoken language and is ready to move on to the written word.

Nonverbal communication: the early months

Mothers and fathers communicate with their baby using many nonverbal tools that come naturally, including facial expressions, tone of voice, and touch. These nonverbal interactions are key in early infancy in helping the baby to regulate his feelings, feelings which at the start are very basic and centred around whether he is feeling comfort or discomfort.

From the first days, the baby is communicating with you through sounds and facial expressions. The key is to quietly give her your attention, listen and respond. This tells the baby that communication is worthwhile, that it gets results, and it shows her how to engage in the back and forth of conversation where listening is as important as talking. Try to talk about what your baby is focussing on (visually). Try and align with your baby and follow her lead: if she smiles and looks at you she is ready to communicate, and if she arches her back, cries or turns her head away she may be signalling she has had enough (not that she doesn't like you!). Communicating when your baby is ready and stopping when she has had enough shows that you value her communication. It is interesting that when a mother or father spends less than 45 minutes a day interacting with a nine-month-old, they tend to underestimate their capabilities and 'baby' them. This makes the interaction less rewarding for both parent and child.

Listening is as important as speaking in communication. Babies can be helped to learn to listen. Try these ideas to encourage good listening:
• Point at things such as a ticking clock, a helicopter overhead, or a bird

singing and say "Listen" to help him focus on the sounds that are all around us
- Talk about the sounds the baby can make, for example when banging things, splashing in the bath, or clapping hands
- Enjoy music, rhymes and rhythm together

Research shows that both fathers and mothers tend to communicate less with boys, which may be one reason for boy's often later development, so consciously 'bucking that trend' can be useful. Also, fathers tend to vocalise less in general, and to be more hesitant about singing and dancing with their child. Since doing this is so valuable, it may be good to recognise self-consciousness and try to get on with it when no-one else is around, until it seems second nature.

> From the first days, the baby is communicating with you through sounds and facial expressions."

Moving towards talking

The young baby needs a good model for spoken language. Montessori believed – and it is now widely accepted – that it was important for the baby to be exposed to adult's conversations and natural speech (that is, between adults, and also older children) in order to pick up the sounds and patterns that make up the child's native language(s). This happens naturally if the baby is kept with his mother or father as they go about their daily life, chatting to a neighbour, answering the phone, talking to older siblings and so on.

The baby also learns from what is called 'parent-ese', which is the natural way grown-ups often speak to babies – and which fathers as well as mothers automatically start to do when talking to their newborn in the minutes after birth. This special way of talking is characterized by:

- a softer, higher pitch
- an almost lilting tone

- repetition of simple phrases and key words
- simplified but basically correct grammar

Note that parent-ese is not the same as baby talk, which is how the toddler may speak when they first begin putting words together (for example, "me no want horsie"). Rather than mimicking baby talk with their child, parents should aim to provide a clear model of speech for the child to absorb by speaking naturally.

As the baby moves towards talking it is important to continue offering lots of examples of meaningful speech. The National Literacy Trust suggests:

- **naming things** (*There goes a helicopter; This is an oak tree*)
- **describing things** (*The kitten is soft and furry isn't she?*)
- **comparing things** (*This rattle is much louder than that one, isn't it?*)
- **explaining things** (*When you push the car, its wheels go round and round to make it zoom along*)
- **giving directions** (*First you open the velcro, then you slide your foot in. Now you pull the strap across and close the velcro; look, now your sandal's on*)

Another excellent source of language is, of course, books. As soon as the baby can focus on pictures and sit in your lap, books with simple illustrations or photographs can be shared and story books will soon follow. Remember that understanding will exceed spoken vocabulary for a long time, so often even very young babies will enjoy sitting and listening to stories. It's important that fathers 'model' interest in books as well as mothers: research shows that there's a clear link between how often a father reads to his infant in the first year and his child's interest in books later.

As we have seen, from the first days of life the baby has enormous potential. The first year is a time of extraordinary growth and development, driven by the baby's innate drive to explore the world around him. Attachment, movement and communication all play key roles. Montessori recognised this potential inherent in the child and developed a philosophy for unlocking it. In the next chapter we will look in more detail at her ideas, and how they can be used today to discover the potential in your child.

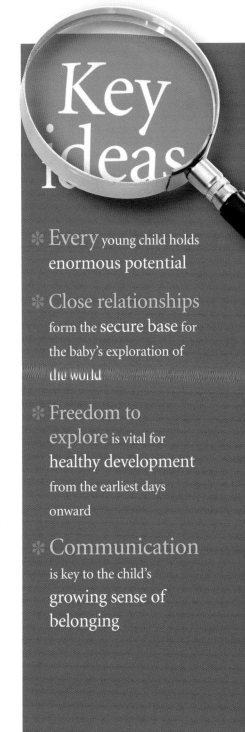

Key ideas

* **Every** young child holds enormous potential

* **Close relationships** form the **secure base** for the baby's exploration of **the world**

* **Freedom to explore** is vital for **healthy development** from the earliest days onward

* **Communication** is key to the child's **growing sense of belonging**

Chapter 2

Unlocking the child's potential

As we have seen, from birth the young child has tremendous potential as an explorer, discoverer and citizen of the world. For parents the key is first of all to simply notice this potential, and a Montessori approach is ideally suited to this all-important task.

So what exactly is the Montessori approach and what can it offer us as parents? You may have heard of Montessori nurseries, but may not have realised that the ideas are not just confined to an educational approach. You do not need to send your child to a Montessori school or buy any special educational materials to benefit from the ideas. Montessori is not exclusive; anyone can bring Montessori ideas into the home to use with their families.

Montessori is a philosophy, a way of thinking and a set of values that can provide an approach to life and parenting. It is based on core attitudes of respect and trust, and simply requires you to slow down, stand back and tune in to the rhythm of your child. It is about understanding that even very young children are driven by a need to be independent and want to take part and be involved in all those rituals of daily living that we often take for granted. We can help by adapting our home and our attitudes to let children become more involved in the everyday tasks that mean so much to them. How many times have you heard a young toddler defiantly insist "me do it!" when an adult tries to help, or seen the look of triumph when he finally manages to do what he set out to do: "I did it!"? There is an enormous rush of self esteem and pride in being allowed and able to 'do it by myself' and this ultimately is what Montessori is all about: respecting each child as an individual and as an active learner, and encouraging all children to reach their fullest potential.

This chapter will look at these core ideas of the Montessori approach in more detail, to give you a basic idea of what this philosophy is all about and start you thinking about how you might incorporate it into your daily family life.

Children raised in a Montessori way "learn to think of the world as an exciting place full of possibilities. They begin to know themselves as powerful people who can do all sorts of things for themselves. They think of adults as helpful friends who are always there if needed, but who never try to overly interfere or control their activities. This is because Montessori teachers [parents] really respect young children as individuals and treat them as dynamic natural learners."

First published in *Montessori International* (2003)

Who was Maria Montessori?

Maria Montessori was in many ways an extraordinary woman. Born in Italy in 1870, she is famous for being the first woman to graduate from the University of Rome with a degree in medicine. After a decade working in medicine and continuing her studies in psychology, education and anthropology, in 1907 Montessori became involved with a pioneering project to teach the poor children of a Rome housing estate, leading to the creation of the first 'Children's House' and in short order international fame for Montessori. She worked tirelessly from that point until her death in 1952 on her approach for educating young children, travelling the world, lecturing, writing and developing the ideas that form the basis of the Montessori philosophy.

'Follow the child'

If the Montessori ethos could be distilled into three words, they would be 'follow the child'.

What makes the Montessori approach special is this overriding focus on letting the child take the lead, on celebrating the uniqueness of each child and his tremendous potential, and on believing in the child as an intrinsically motivated natural learner. Montessori's observations of children led her to the conclusion that the child is naturally motivated to fulfil his potential and become independent; our role as adults is to support the child as an active learner, to 'help me to do it for myself', a process that begins at birth.

> *Montessori, I believe, offers a counterbalance to the modern disease of image over substance and allows children to judge themselves against their own standards rather than the expectations of others. From the very start Montessori told us that the child is saying "help me to help myself"... Not only does the child develop the functional capability of doing things for him/herself, s/he also develops the self-belief in his/her own ability.*

Chris Manville, first published in *Montessori International* (2010)

Given the opportunity to act freely and choose her own activity, the child will actively pursue new challenges. The key for the adult is to create an appropriate environment and then leave the child undisturbed to pursue what is currently alive or meaningful for her, whatever that

Finding your own way as a parent

I feel lucky to have had two bites at the parenting cherry. I had my first son when I was just 17 and raised him as a single mother. Now 12 years later I find myself married and with a beautiful new baby girl. Everybody wanted to give me advice as a teenage mum, but I had to find my own way. It felt overwhelming at times but now I realise all new parents feel like that, not just young parents. Sometimes I felt a bit different to the other mums I met at the baby drop-ins but like every other parent I loved my baby and wanted the best for him. I felt at the time that I had something to prove and now realise that was a big waste of time. Being a parent is a bit of a leveller - we are all in it together and need to take whatever support we can. My son got a place at a local Montessori nursery and I found out a bit about it by talking to the teachers and sitting in on some of the sessions. I found it helped me relax, stand back and try and tune in with him a bit more, find out what he was interested in and go with that. Now with my daughter I feel much more laid back about parenting and am really enjoying spending time with her. It doesn't matter how old you are, whether there are one parents or two, my advice is trust yourself, listen to everyone and take what works for you, but most importantly listen to yourself and to your baby and do it your way.

Tonia, mother of two, ages 6 months and 12

may be, and in this way to respect the inner spirit of the child as a unique individual. Even as a baby, the child does not need to be entertained or engaged by an adult all or even most of the time; her natural instincts will lead her to explore the world around her and add to her knowledge of how things work in it.

When a child has freely chosen what he is doing, he will often enter into a deep spell of concentration that may last several minutes or several hours – this 'state of flow' is at the heart of child-centred learning; when the child is concentrating in this way the most important thing a parent can do is nothing! Simply observe, without interrupting with conversation, questions, or offers of help. These observations will give you new insight into what the child's interests are as well as what sort of new challenges to offer in order to create an environment that will support his development in all areas.

> **During a sensitive period the child can absorb much more, naturally and easily, than would be the case at another time."**

Windows of opportunity: the 'sensitive periods'

Montessori's observations of children led her to develop the idea that each child passes through what she called 'sensitive periods' for learning different things; these are like a window of opportunity, when a child is completely ready and open to learn something new.

As a father or mother be on the look-out for these opportunities and take full advantage, as during a sensitive period the child can absorb much more, naturally and easily, than would be the case at another time; a skill can be learned either before or after the natural sensitive period, but not as easily and not to such a full, deep extent. The sensitive period for learning a language is a common example: a child's language develops rapidly between birth and age six, with an 'explosion' of spoken language between around 18 months and three years. If a child is raised bilingually she will easily and naturally absorb a second language (or even a third!) in this time, but if a second language is introduced later in life, after this window of opportunity has gone, it can certainly be learned but with far more effort and never to the same authentically bilingual extent.

How can you recognise a sensitive period? From infancy onwards the child will pass through stages where you will notice that she

- becomes very interested in certain objects or activities (such as solid food for babies ready to be weaned, using the toilet for toddlers or learning to read and write for older children)
- begins to focus on one thing with intense concentration
- repeats the same thing over and over (this could be anything from going up or down stairs to putting on shoes to collecting tiny pebbles)

The key for the parent is to wait and watch, then give your child plenty of time to explore whatever it is that is inspiring him. This can require tremendous patience at times – your child may wish to stop and look at every single tiny pebble along the walk home, or to take his shoes off in order to put them back on again several times just as you are trying to leave the house! It can be useful, when you find yourself impatient and wanting to rush the child, to 'catch yourself' and consider whether, at this point in time, you really do need to rush. Sometimes you do; sometimes you don't.

The child's natural drive toward independence

Recently it was brought home to me very clearly not just how important the freedom to do tasks for herself is to my daughter Mia, but also what an increasing and powerful desire she has to be independent in the home. When she began asking for drinks we would simply go to the kitchen and pour a cup of milk. One day, after seeing this happen a few times, she got the carton of milk out of the fridge herself and took it to the lounge, helpfully declaring "Me want drink milk". It was lovely to see her being able to join in with a normal everyday activity. We moved her cups to a lower cupboard so that she was able to get everything she needed ready before asking for help with unscrewing the lid and pouring the milk.

Of course, what happened next should not have been a surprise considering that not only do children watch and take in what adults do with incredible detail, but that they are also very inclined to solve their own problems. Mia had gone to

get a drink – she had fetched her cup out of the cupboard and then opened the fridge. Unable to open the screw top milk carton herself she then did what she saw me doing when I make coffee, which is to use the milk bottle instead. Unfortunately a full pint is quite tricky to handle for a girl who has just turned two, and makes a surprisingly large puddle on the floor once it has been turned upside down. Undeterred, she made a good attempt at mopping it up with a tea towel before coming to tell me "Daddy, milk on floor". The joy of seeing my sturdy independent little girl solving problems for herself far outweighed any disappointment over the prospect of only black coffee for the rest of the day! Anyway, after we had mopped up we went for a very pleasant daughter and dad walk to the shop to buy some more milk. Naturally, I let Mia hand the coins to the cashier – she wouldn't want it any other way.

Jeremy, Montessori teacher and father of two, ages 2 and 8

The sensitive periods

> " In the first years of life, the child is in a sensitive period for exploring the world using the five senses."

Observing your six-month-old, for example, you might see that she enjoys lying on her tummy and when you place a favourite rattle just out of reach she really struggles to reach it and seems delighted to finally get hold of it, shaking it vigorously and listening to its sound. This is a typical example of young babies' innate curiosity supported by their need to move and explore. In the first years of life, the child is in a sensitive period for exploring the world using the five senses (which is why so many things will find their way into her mouth!), and also a sensitive period for movement, specifically developing gross motor skills to allow her to roll over, sit up, crawl and eventually pull herself up to standing and begin to walk. The sensitive period for movement also extends into balance, hand-eye coordination and fine motor skills.

Observing your toddler, you may notice that they go through a stage of asking for objects to be named again and again: "What's this? What's this? What's this?". This is a typical example of a child in his sensitive period for language, here spoken language, but later on written language as well. The child has worked out that words designate specific things and is gathering information about which words we use to describe different things. This will soon blossom into spoken language, with the child incorporating this new vocabulary into his own speech.

During the early years, other sensitive periods include the sensitive period for order (observe a toddler matching shoes at the shoe shelf, or becoming inconsolable when an object has been moved from what the child perceives to be its rightful place), the sensitive period for small objects (many small children love to collect tiny things to keep in a special tin or small box) and from around two and a half till six, a sensitive period for social skills, coinciding with the start of nursery/school, and first friendships.

A Montessori-inspired environment

So what does a Montessori environment look like? The following chapters contain lots of practical ideas that you can try out with your child/ren in your own home, all of which are based around the idea of 'following the child'. A Montessori-inspired space:

- provides opportunities that are meaningful for the child or children who are using it
- contains beautiful, interesting objects and activities, so the child is drawn in
- is calm, so the child can focus
- is accessible and orderly, so the child can find whatever she needs and return it to its place when she has finished with it

" ...the first lesson we must learn is that the tiny child's absorbent mind finds all its nutriment in its surroundings. Here it has to locate itself and build itself up from what it takes in. Especially at the beginning of life we must, therefore, make the environment as interesting and attractive as we can."

Maria Montessori
(The Absorbent Mind)

No special equipment is necessary to create this type of environment for your baby or child; it is all about your approach to the space you have available and to providing opportunities that will be meaningful for your child – this is often as simple, for example, as noticing that a toddler is enjoying putting lids on things and taking them off again, going through the recycling bin and kitchen cupboards to find more containers with lids and putting them out for the child to explore. Or watching your five-year-old and a friend use sticks, buckets of water and string to devise 'traps' in the garden, having a rummage through the junk drawer and leaving out some elastic bands, bungee cords, or old planks of wood for the inventors to find and use however they see fit.

> **Did you know that the founders of Google, Amazon and Wikipedia all started with a Montessori education and so did Sean Combs, better known as 'P Diddy'?**
>
> *Wall Street Journal*, 5th April, 2011

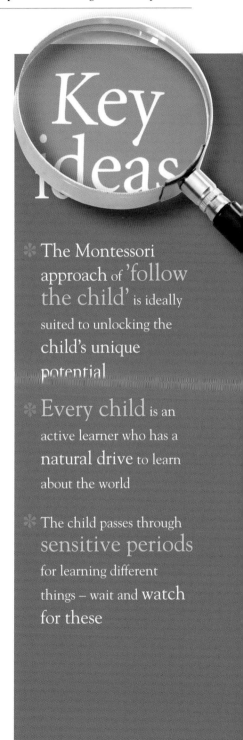

Key ideas

* The Montessori approach of 'follow the child' is ideally suited to unlocking the child's unique potential

* Every child is an active learner who has a natural drive to learn about the world

* The child passes through sensitive periods for learning different things – wait and watch for these

Chapter 3

A Montessori way of life

This chapter will give you some practical ideas and look more broadly at interacting, exploring and creating with your child in keeping with the Montessori philosophy of 'follow the child'. As a mother or father you can offer so much to your child just by being in tune with her, responding to her needs, reacting to her interests, answering her questions and taking things at her pace. There is no need to buy the latest toys or games, or sign up for lots of organised activities, to offer your child a rich tapestry of experiences.

Freedom to move and explore

Montessori advised parents to take babies outdoors and into the world, to experience as much as possible at their parent's side, and this remains good advice. Think about how you carry your baby, to allow as full a view as possible of both the world and you. For the very young baby a sling is ideal as it gives the baby an excellent view of what is happening while still feeling safe and secure in contact with you. When not in use as a carrier many slings can be used as a mat on the floor to give your baby a place to explore and move freely no matter where you are. As the months pass slings can be adapted to carry the growing baby on your hip or on your back. Babies can often spend a lot of their time being moved from highchair to car seat to buggy and back again, all of which restrain

Montessori in the city

It is never too late to introduce a child to the Montessori method. It is a way of life that is surprisingly accessible and can be practised at any time and any location. I live in an urban area where nature and quietness have taken a backseat. Despite this the Montessori method has made me think differently about parenting and made me slow right down to my children's pace. I learned that it is possible to create islands of calm and real learning in a sea of traffic jams, television and school runs. Often when I take Finn for walks in his stroller he would be still and stare at trees or his hands and, as advised in some of my reading material, I just let him be.

My appeal to all parents is to take what you can from Montessori's teachings. Show your child little, natural things. Allow quiet reflection and concentration that even in the busiest of cities could be as simple as turning off the television more or even allowing your child to finish that puzzle in silence without distraction for ten minutes.

Charlotte Stokes, first published in *Montessori International* (2011)

and restrict movement, so try to give the baby as much freedom of movement as possible, allowing lots of time on both tummy and back for good muscle development.

Spending time outdoors is important for children at all ages. Free, unstructured time outdoors gives children valuable opportunities to explore and move. With all this freedom it can sometimes be hard to know when to intervene and it is often a fine line between making sure your child is safe while also giving enough freedom to explore independently and opportunities to take risks. No parent gets it right all the time!

Unstructured time to play outdoors also allows the child to develop a sense of how living things are interconnected. This sense of wonder and awe can easily equal that created by electronic games or fantasy movies, if given the chance – having only ever seen them in books, I still remember the look of amazement and pure joy on my son's face the first time he saw a real elephant.

Building on this freedom of movement is the freedom:

- to explore and do without interruption
- to enjoy the process and do it their own way
- to perhaps struggle a bit before working out a solution without being helped straightaway
- to just work in silence, without distractions such as a parent constantly asking questions or offering more information, or background noises such as TV

Letting your child take risks

I remember not letting my first child have a go at a metal chain bridge at our local park until he was nearly four, telling him it was "for big kids" (the bridge is about four feet off the ground and very wobbly). When I did finally let him have a go I walked next to him so I could help him if he got stuck or started to fall through, but in fact I later realised that this 'helping hand' was also a message that I wasn't confident that he could manage it on his own. With my second and third children I made a conscious decision to be more hands off and let them take risks when they were ready. They were up and across the bridge around the age of two!

Exploring outdoors

In some ways we were lucky that Mia was born in the summer as that enabled her to be outside from a very young age, lying on the grass whilst we still had warm days. We were quite keen to get her onto the grass as this was not something we had done with our first child. I remember how careful we were to always sit him on a blanket whilst in the garden or at the park, and how he would happily stay on it without venturing more than a hand or a foot onto the grass.

Looking back we had unwittingly given him the impression that it was not alright for him to be on the grass, because we were careful to keep him off it. This is why we did things differently with Mia. As she began crawling around outside we did find that she was often getting her clothes wet and muddy, although this was not really a problem for her, and I didn't mind at all; I soon learnt which clothes her Mum didn't want her exploring outside in! I did have to be alert to her eating grass, mud, worms, soil and the like, but this phase

didn't last too long. The value of her being able to freely explore the new textures and sensations she found outside was well worth her getting mucky. And of course, the muck itself was something new for her to discover.

When we go to parks with Mia it really is a new adventure every time, and not just for her. I love to let her explore freely, choosing her own route and going at her speed. Sometimes I do need to intervene – if she is about to trip and fall, or disappear down a ditch. It can be tough to just let her go, the natural reaction being to keep your child as safe a possible, but she can only show me what her capabilities are if I let her have a go. I am now expert at shadowing her with a following hand ready to catch, but not holding on. I need to be, as she is so determined to do things by herself, she will demand that I let go – often accompanied by that quintessential Montessori phrase "Let me do it me self!".

Jeremy, Montessori teacher and father of two, ages 2 and 8

Hard as it can be, often the best thing you can do as a parent is nothing. You can help your child develop problem-solving skills by not jumping in when he seems to be struggling or unsure what to do next. Unless your child is becoming overly frustrated, wait and watch and see what happens next. If you are asked for help, consider whether you might offer resources, encouragement (*"That is quite tricky because there are lots of blue pieces in that puzzle; you're really sticking with it"*) or hints rather than either doing it for him or giving him the answer.

In order to get the most from the activities they choose themselves, children need to know that they have the freedom to choose their own activity and then the time to do it properly (whatever that means for them). By resisting the temptation to schedule lots of activities at set times, you give your child the gift of extended periods of free time so she can:

- find activities that inspire, captivate and challenge her
- repeat/continue with these activities as long as she wishes
- get into a state of deep concentration or 'flow'
- move through feeling "I'm bored" on her own, without being told what to do next

Engaging the child with the routines of living

Often the learning our children are doing, naturally, independently, on a day-to-day basis, goes almost unnoticed in the flurry of daily life. But in fact it is just those day-to-day activities that create the authentic context where so much learning is taking place.

Look for example at a toddler getting ready to go to nursery in the morning. If you had time to stop and watch, you might see her:

- getting dressed
- eating cereal and drinking a glass of milk
- brushing teeth, washing hands and using the toilet
- putting on shoes and socks
- packing a bag to take
- leaving the house on foot, by bike or by car

Just a typical morning, happening in more or less the same way all over the country. So what is your child learning through this fairly ordinary routine? And how can you as a mother or father help her to 'do it herself'? Generally speaking, the best thing the parent can do is be patient, and allow enough time for the child to do things independently without being rushed (often easier said than done, as I well know).

Here are just some of the things the child is learning in this typical morning routine:

- **getting dressed:** To encourage independence, your child can choose what to wear, possibly from a selection. I sometimes offer a weather report in the morning and suggest for example short sleeves or long sleeves, shorts or trousers, etc. The actual act of getting dressed requires quite complex gross and fine motor skills.
- **eating cereal and drinking a glass of milk:** Again, your child can be encouraged to choose what to eat and drink (possibly from a limited selection) and allowed to get the bowl, spoon and cup from the cupboard or shelf before pouring the cereal and drink independently. Pouring cereal or milk helps develop a sense of quantity: how much will fit in the bowl or cup? How much is a serving? How much milk do I want on my cereal? Eating with a spoon develops good fine motor

skills and coordination as does managing a cup with no lid – any spills can be cleaned up by the child, who can be shown where the cloth for spills is kept and how to rinse it out.

- **brushing teeth, washing hands and using the toilet:** These basic tasks are fundamental to the child's independence. The key for the parent is to be present enough to help out when needed or offer a gentle reminder when a step has been forgotten, but hands-off enough to let the child do it independently.

- **putting on shoes and socks:** Again this develops fine motor skills. Shoes for young children are often quite straightforward to do up, either with Velcro tabs or slip-ons, so it is relatively easy for even quite young children to start doing this on their own. Finding a pair also builds matching skills and helps develop the child's sense of one-to-one correspondence (one shoe for one foot, two shoes for two feet), both of which relate to very early mathematical thinking.

- **packing a bag to take:** Children have a natural sense of order and will often enjoy making sure they have everything they need for nursery. You could use a picture list hung on the wall to refer to as a prompt. This gives your child a sense of independence and responsibility from the outset.

- **leaving the house on foot, by bike or by car:** Here your child is practicing gross motor skills as well as orientating spatially to the local area and getting to know the route to familiar places.

The role of the adult here is partly logistical, creating an environment where your child can access what he needs and function independently. This could mean, for example, having low hooks, a dedicated cupboard or shelf in the kitchen, a step stool in the bathroom, a manageable

" ...your child can be encouraged to choose what to eat and drink (possibly from a limited selection) and allowed to get the bowl, spoon and cup from the cupboard."

system for finding clean clothes and so on. Also think about providing easy access to the tools to use when things go wrong, such as cloths for spills or a small dustpan and brush.

But as a mother or father you also play a crucial role as a sort of 'tech support', constantly moving in the background making sure things are running smoothly. This role takes practice and patience; nobody gets it right all the time. Some ideas to think about:

- Give clear, step-by-step instructions on how to do something, such as pouring cereal into a bowl or washing hands, and be prepared to repeat them as often as necessary.

- Model but also explain polite behaviour, for example how to greet visitors or the table manners that are important in your house, and again, be prepared to repeat the 'lesson'.

- Allow enough time for your child to do it by himself without being rushed. I try to build an extra 15 minutes in between the time when all the bags are packed and ready and 'all' we have left to do is 'toilet checks and shoes' and the time when I want to actually leave the house, but with three young children this isn't always enough!

- Be patient and try to let your child do things on her own without intervening, but at the same time be ready to step in with a helping hand, before frustration takes over.

- Try not to be tempted to do something for your child to get a faster or better result. Remind yourself that the child is learning and that things may not be perfect the first time around, but that the effort being made is more important than the end result.

- If things are starting to go a bit pear-shaped, simple things such as breathing regularly and relaxing your shoulders can sometimes make a bigger difference than you might think.

- Think about your own attitude to household tasks and the message that sends your child. Where is the line between work and play? What can you do to make it fun? Young children often enjoy the process of household chores as toddlers but then pick up on the adult attitude that these jobs are 'dull', 'a chore' or 'something we have to do before we can play' and start to resist helping out. Think about including children not serving children, even from a very young age.

Including children in daily tasks

As our children have grown they have been encouraged to think of our family as a team of equal players and that we all need to help each other out and share the responsibility to get things done. We divide up tasks and everyone has things they prefer to do; washing the floor, washing the car and raking leaves are popular, dusting less so!

Laying the table, pouring drinks, clearing plates and loading the dishwasher have all become part of the process of mealtimes; it does not end when we have finished eating, but when the table and kitchen are clear. Cooking is a favourite activity, but there is also a mutually understood end point that comes after the washing up! I have come to believe that the more you include children in these simple, everyday tasks the more mutual respect we all feel for each other. It is just part of life, part of the rhythm of everyday living.

You need to show children how to do things, clearly and simply, but give them scope to do it their way and learn by making mistakes. I try not to interfere, even if this sometimes means biting my tongue or sitting on my hands.

The rewards are less resentful parents, less of the 'I have to do everything!' feeling. The children feel empowered by taking on responsibility, proud to be making a contribution. I hope that they carry these attitudes forward with them as they grow.
Sophie, mother of three, ages 2, 7 and 10

Managing time

As your baby becomes a toddler it can be very helpful to include him in how you manage time. This might include making short checklists of morning and evening routines, so for example our family's morning routine checklist is posted on the fridge and simply lists:

- eat breakfast
- get dressed
- brush teeth
- make bed

The children are free to do these in any order as long as they are done before they go to play; my middle son always gets dressed as soon as his feet touch the floor in the morning, whereas my eldest prefers to do everything else first then get dressed. Even my youngest, a toddler, will check the list and remind her brothers "morning routine boys" if they get distracted, but increasingly these simple tasks are becoming habits and so they just get done, more or less automatically. We also have a family whiteboard that shows that week's activities, the planned dinners for the week (each family member contributes ideas for this), and sometimes a short 'to do' list. I also use a large family calendar and the children know they can check that as well to see what is coming up, whose birthday is next or when we are free if they want to invite a friend round. When they were younger we had a simple weekly wall chart that showed our regular activities on the day of the week, but as they got older this was too basic.

These are ideas that have worked for our family but there is no one

> "The key is to find a system that works for you and then get your child involved. In this way the information is shared, expectations are clear, and routines are predictable and consistent, but still flexible."

 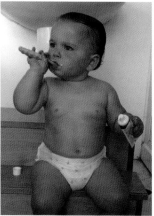 

'right way' to do this and often the systems change over time; the key is to find a system that works for you and then get your child involved. In this way the information is shared, expectations are clear, and routines are predictable and consistent, but still flexible.

Interestingly, it is during the child's third year that the hippocampus develops in the brain which enables them to understand a chronology of events – things that happened before now, things that will come later. Children aged between two and three start to become interested in retelling things that happened in their past, and in hearing you retell things that happened to them (often over and over again!). They now have a personal store of memories to recall and celebrate, and can look forward to things in the future. The calendar is a great tool for this as it shows both what has happened and what is coming up. Other practical ideas are looking at family photos together, making picture timelines of family holidays or other events, and celebrating birthdays with a picture collage of the child's past birthdays starting with 'year zero'.

Out and about

There are now so many 'child friendly' attractions, play groups and activities for toddlers and young children on offer to parents that it can be tempting to over-schedule your child's time. There is real social value in making contact with other parents for mutual support and also to allow your child to socialise and develop certain skills. But when you are in connection with your child, communicating together, explaining things and responding to questions, wherever you go and whatever you do together will be meaningful. Joining in with 'ordinary' trips that need to be done like walking to the post box to post a letter, going to the shops, taking the car in to be serviced, going on a bus or going to the library to choose a new book will all be significant and meaningful for your child, as long as they are viewed that way and not as chores to be done before the fun can start.

'Just' going for regular walks around your neighbourhood or local area with an interested adult is often the best entertainment for a child of any age. Walking at the child's pace, with no destination in mind or errand to be run, exploring whatever takes the child's interest, repeating things

Going for walks

At 18 months old, Lincoln just loves exploring our neighbourhood on foot, and we make this our main activity on our days together. Rather than heading out of our gate to somewhere specific, I follow Lincoln's lead, letting him set the pace and direction. Our 'somewhere specific' comes every few steps when he makes his next discovery, whether it be the cover of a water main, a daisy, a pathway, a wall to balance on or a puddle to splash in, and we continue on in this way until I can see he is ready to come back home.

There are times when I ask myself (and am also asked by others) "what is so different about taking a Montessori approach to parenting?" Using this example of walking with Lincoln, at face value I would probably say there is nothing different. We are certainly not the only toddler and parent out walking, and I would have walked with my child even if I had never discovered Dr Montessori's writings. However, what I think is different is the value that I place on this activity because of what Dr Montessori revealed about the nature of childhood and how best to support the child's natural development. Our exploring time is not just about getting fresh air or soaking up time and it is certainly about far more than just exercising his legs. My knowledge of the Montessori approach helps me identify Lincoln's current needs, interests and sensitive periods. I know that he has a real need to be active and practise his body movements with lots of repetition as well as increasing his level of challenge. He loves to make his own choices and discoveries and uses all of his senses to learn about his world. He is very social and enjoys practising greeting people (social graces), and is just beginning to want to have a name assigned to all the things he encounters. I truly believe he is able to drive his own development and so I find it really reassuring that the one activity that meets all of these needs at the same time is the activity that perhaps brings him the most joy.

Tessa McTaylor, first published in *Montessori Voices* (Dec 2009)

Here are some other ideas for simple, fun things you can do with your child 'out and about':

- play outdoor games: fly kites, blow bubbles, play catch
- go on bike rides around your neighbourhood or local area
- follow a map of your neighbourhood/local area or make your own
- shop for the ingredients and cook a special treat or meal
- get the bus to a local garden centre
- have a picnic with some friends
- find a good tree to climb

and finding new things every time, seeing similarities and differences on different days, can show the child amazing things about how the world around him works. I have very happy memories of walking around the block with my grandfather (and sometimes other family members) every night after dinner; I clearly remember examining cracks in the sidewalk and looking forward to the place where a dog had run through the wet concrete leaving a trail of paw prints, and also the excitement that I felt when, very occasionally, we would set out in the opposite direction and walk the same walk the other way. Try walking without talking unless your child starts a conversation or asks a question and see what happens. Children love to stop and notice small details; just let them experience, touch, smell, see whatever it is that has captivated their interest. At any age they will naturally gravitate towards what is 'alive' for them at the moment -- light, colours, shapes, letters on signs, animals, digging a hole, collecting leaves.

Promoting positive behaviour

A Montessori-inspired approach to parenting starts from a base of mutual respect and trust between each parent and their child, and between the child's parents and other key caregivers. By respecting children as individuals and responding to their needs accordingly, you create a bond that demonstrates to your children that they are understood, that they will be helped when help is needed and most importantly, that they are loved. It is very important that both parents do this. A good relationship with one parent can be undermined by a poor relationship with the other – or between the parents. The quality of the parents' own relationship has an enormous impact on their children.

Team parenting

Researchers are just beginning to understand the importance of parents' developing a strong parenting team. This means both parents feeling confident and skilled in interacting with their children, and often means renegotiation of caring/earning roles so the child gets to spend sufficient time with each parent. Team parenting also depends on parents' willingness and ability to acknowledge and deal with difference and disagreement. No parent is 'always right'.

Tips for communicating effectively

- Behaviour is communication. Observe your child. What provokes different types of behaviour? How do you respond? What happens next? Sometimes children learn through cause and effect 'what buttons to press' to gain responses from adults. Make sure you give plenty of positive attention to your child.

- Allow sufficient time for the child to do what he needs to do, and also to process requests you make.

- Use positive language and offer a positive alternative. Show the child what you want her to do, so if your child is throwing her books on the floor try, "*We read books; if you want to throw something we can go outside and throw your ball. First let's pick up your books together.*"

- Try not to ask a question you don't want an answer to! So, if it's bath time and no amount of negotiating is going to change that, say "*Let's go have a bath*" instead of "*Do you want a bath?*"

- Try to say 'yes' as much as possible, sometimes even when you mean no ("*Yes you can have that, as soon as your brother finishes with it*" instead of "*No, your brother is playing with it, you have to wait*").

- Save the word "no" for when you really need it (when the child is in danger, or someone could get hurt, or something is about to be broken), so the child will learn that no really means no. Also try to explain why you have said no in simple terms so the child understands what is being refused and why.

Freedom and boundaries

I am sometimes frustrated when my two year old daughter refuses to 'do as she is told'. At the moment this often seems to happen when I ask her to get her coat and shoes on, and she would rather keep doing whatever she is doing. It can be especially maddening if we are going to be late as a result, and if we are out and about I can start to doubt myself as a parent when I'm not getting the results I want. When I try being firmer, it often escalates into a battle of wills, which by its nature has to have a winner and a loser, and as anyone with a two year old can tell you, that will is incredibly strong.

When it is all going a bit wrong, I try to take a deep breath and remind myself that toddlers do not need 'taming' as if they are wild animals; we do not want to break their spirit. Instead I like to see children who are assertive, at times even feisty, and who are aware of their own needs, but who can also cooperate with others. A strong bond and a loving relationship support young children to want to do things for other people rather than just respond to their own needs. But this happens slowly and over time.

One of Montessori's key principles is freedom for the child, but this is a freedom with boundaries. It is frightening for a child of any age to have no boundaries, so rather than 'impose discipline', it is important to think about creating consistent boundaries. Along with boundaries, routines and predictability also help a child feel emotionally secure. Knowing what happens next is comforting and knowing what is expected of you and what to expect from others leads to a feeling of security. Young children don't need a whole lot of surprises. What they need is for tomorrow to be very like yesterday, punctuated by your family's own comforting routines – play, meals, a walk to the shops, bath, stories, bed.

Rewards and punishments

It is interesting to note that Montessori did not believe in rewards or punishments, as she believed this interfered with children's own natural desire to learn, to socialise, and to reach their full potential. Montessori believed in setting clear and simple ground rules. In our house there are only two rules: respect other people and respect your surroundings.

When behaviour falls short, we can easily and simply explain how what has happened either does not respect others or does not respect the surroundings, so that next time the child will have more information about what is expected. If parents have high expectations and set clear ground rules then children can feel secure in the knowledge that they know what is expected and will, over time, learn how to behave accordingly.

Tips for promoting positive behaviour

- Actively encourage decision making by letting children make decisions about the little but important things in their lives. This helps

them to be more independent and feel they have some control, rather than feeling they are being told what to do all the time.

- Different strategies work with different ages. At two, distraction is often the best tactic. Try and ignore most of the behaviour you disapprove of and give positive attention to the behaviour you do like (*Look how happy Rashmi is when you help her build her tower!*).

- Let your child take some (acceptable) risks and learn about natural consequences by themselves, so for example, if your child throws something on the floor it may break, or if your child chooses not to eat at lunch time he will probably feel hungry later in the afternoon.

- If you feel you are losing it walk away! The things you do and say when you are angry are unlikely to be helpful and an adult who has lost control is very frightening for a child.

- Always attend to physical needs first – often children melt down because they are hungry, thirsty or tired; fix that and you will hopefully be well on your way back to peace. Try to carry a water bottle and snack wherever you go – small children need to eat little and often to keep their blood sugar levels up.

- Balance active times and quieter activities; in the home keep space set aside for both so your child can move between them as needed, for example by perhaps having a small trampoline to bounce on along with a cosy reading area with beanbags and cushions.

- When dealing with more than one child keep in mind that 'fair' does not necessarily mean 'equal' – each child is unique with different needs.

Above all, try to remember that adults, particularly mothers and fathers, are the greatest role models for young children. They will copy you, look up to you, and emulate you, so try and be aware of yourself as a role model. It's not what you say, but what you do that has the greatest impact. Keep in mind that no approach works perfectly every day and in every situation – Montessori isn't a magic wand! It takes time, patience and effort to establish a rhythm of living that suits your family. There will be ups and downs, and of course family life is constantly changing and evolving as children grow and change, so what works for a while will need to be continually reviewed and updated. But if you start from a base of mutual respect and support, things will tend to fall into place.

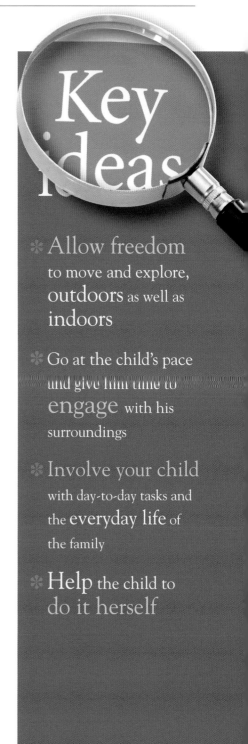

Key ideas

✳ Allow freedom to move and explore, outdoors as well as indoors

✳ Go at the child's pace and give him time to engage with his surroundings

✳ Involve your child with day-to-day tasks and the everyday life of the family

✳ Help the child to do it herself

Chapter 4

Creating a Montessori-inspired living space

This chapter will look at different areas in the home, both indoors and outdoors, and consider practical things that you may want to try in each area to nurture the child's potential, at different ages and at different stages of development.

Of course every family is different and every living space is different, so these ideas are meant as a starting point rather than a checklist: a selection of practical suggestions to start you thinking about how you could make your home more 'Montessori'. This does not mean converting your home into a Montessori classroom, or buying any specialist Montessori equipment or activities. It does not even necessarily mean that your house will look that different from anyone else's house (ours certainly doesn't). It simply means following your child, the active learner, on her path, and encouraging her independence.

As always start with your child/children: first, choose a room/area and simply observe how they use the space:

- Does it allow mobility, the freedom to move, explore, and choose?
- Are the things the child needs within reach?
- Are the things the child needs well organised and easy to locate?

Often a small change can make a big difference in how children use a space; think about what you want them to get out of the space and make adjustments accordingly.

A child's eye view

Take a minute and get down on your hands and knees; try seeing the world from a young child's level. You will see a world of knees, edges of sofas and chairs luring you temptingly to climb them, cupboards that entice exploration, drawers that are asking to be pulled out. Also notice what is literally out of sight and out of reach. In the bathroom can you reach the sink to wash your hands? or the towel to dry them? Can you reach your books? Are there also things you can reach that should perhaps be out of bounds?

Try having a conversation with an adult who is standing up while you kneel on the floor: how does it feel to 'talk up to someone' and how does it feel to have a big person 'talk down to you'? Now get the adult to come down and kneel with you on the floor: how does it now feel to have someone talking to you at your level? This is the daily experience of a child, who lives in a world of giants who often talk literally 'right over her head'. Make a point of getting down to your child's level, make eye contact and show her that you are giving her your full attention; you may be surprised at what a difference this change in perspective can make.

A Montessori-inspired bedroom

Infants and toddlers

Sleeping

As we have seen, from the earliest days and weeks freedom of movement for the new baby is crucial. Instead of a cot, you could consider placing a low bed, futon or mattress on the floor or slats (one easy option is to use a child-size mattress that can later go on the child's bed); this is common practice in other parts of the world such as Japan. This low bed allows infants plenty of room to move safely as they explore their surroundings, initially with the smaller movements of the newborn and later rolling over and eventually crawling and walking. With a mattress on the floor, it is also possible to lie next to the child while they are getting off to sleep or if they wake in the night.

The floor bed

What intrigues people about the floor bed? What mystery does it hold?

I never understood why people were so surprised or confused about it. In our home it was almost like people didn't know what to say. I wonder what they were thinking... does the child sleep here, on the floor, can't they afford a crib, a cot? When new people came to our home I found myself trying to explain it. Was I trying to justify our decision, was I trying to educate our guests?

My first son Caspar used a floor bed from around six months. The first six months he slept in a cot... next to my bed. When using the floor bed my main concern was that he would fall out and then when older start wandering around the house getting up to mischief. He never fell out and the only time he got out of his bed was to get into ours.

The floor bed made sense to us. It was easier. I know it doesn't work for everyone and I respect parents who decide otherwise.

For our next baby, the plan is the same. I expect the baby to

sleep at night in the cot next to me until he is around six months, then into the floor bed. I do plan for the baby to use the floor bed during the day almost from the start, at least to lie and play, and this is where I think I will hang our mobiles...

... If you are wondering, for the floor bed we simply use a single bed mattress directly on the floor. Works for us.

from **Kylie D'Alton's** blog How-We-Montessori

Visual stimulation

A mirror on the wall at baby's eye level, possibly alongside the floor bed, is endlessly engaging. The child can get feedback on what her body and face is doing as she moves, and by lying on her stomach to look at the reflection, she is strengthening leg, arm and neck muscles.

For visual stimulation, choose a space with as much natural light as possible so that the new baby can acclimate himself to the changes in light and start to differentiate times of day.

Also for visual stimulation, a mobile hung above the bed or changing mat is ideal. At first the newborn cannot focus on things that are too far away so a mobile should hang around 30cm above the baby. In the first month or so, contrast is good to help the newborn focus, so many mobiles for this age are made up of black and white (and possibly red) shapes and patterns. Later a wider range of colours can be discerned and enjoyed. Mobiles can be bought but are also relatively easy to make by hand or using patterns and tutorials available online; for ideas look at

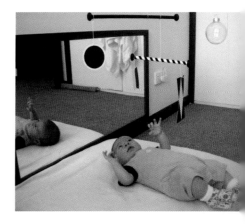

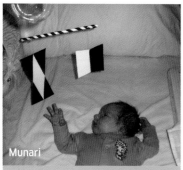

Munari

Baby mobiles

One day after Finn was born I placed the Munari [mobile] within his vision. He immediately noticed it and turned his head to watch it. After this, I would often place him beneath it and he would focus on it whilst remaining quiet but alert; this encouraged him to concentrate. I changed the mobile as Finn became familiarised to it, and as his development progressed I introduced the Gobbi mobile. This mobile encourages a baby to reach out and bat the spheres with his hands, and so making him aware that he is able to affect his environment through movement. I also found wonderful grasping rattles to encourage early work with his hands.

Charlotte Stokes, first published in *Montessori International* (2011)

Gobbi

Munari and Gobbi mobiles which were designed by Montessorians and cater specifically to these very early stages of development.

From around three months, you will be able to observe the baby reaching out to try to touch the mobile (or kick it!) and make it move. In the baby's look of concentration and excitement when she finally touches the mobile, you will see the beginning of the baby's realisation that she has the ability to make things happen in the world around her, a huge developmental leap.

Older children

The older child will obviously have more input over his bedroom and its décor than the infant. Think about things like allowing the child to choose bedding, a colour scheme for the walls or pictures to hang. Look at the room from the child's perspective; can he reach the light switch? Can he turn on music or stories to listen to? Is there a place for him to keep special objects? This can be especially important if they share a room; my two boys each have a set of canvas pockets that hang on their bunk bed that are for their own special things (and strictly off limits for the rest of us!)

Consider whether you want toys kept in the bedroom or whether it is a place just for relaxation/sleep, in which case you may decide to have only books and possibly comfort objects such as cuddly toys in the bedroom. Obviously space considerations have to be taken into account when making this decision.

Looking at the child's clothes, think in terms of independence and access:

- Can he easily reach all the clothes he needs?
- Are they organised in a way that the child can choose outfits that are appropriate for the weather, or different occasions?
- Are most things easy to fasten so he can dress himself without asking for help?
- Is there a clear system for laundry so children can join in easily, starting by putting their dirty clothes in the right place and moving towards folding and putting away their own clothes and eventually starting their own loads of laundry? This may seem ambitious but if you show them how to do it step-by-step and let them do it themselves from beginning to end they will soon get the hang of it.

> " Look at the room from the child's perspective; can he reach the light switch? Can he turn on music or stories to listen to? Is there a place for him to keep special objects?"

A Montessori-inspired living room/play area

Early play: engaging the senses

Baby's first playground

The baby is naturally curious, getting to know first the people closest to her, and then exploring her surroundings. All the very young baby needs is a blanket or soft mat to lie on. This first simple playground gives the baby:

- freedom to move
- the flexibility to be 'where the action is' as the blanket or mat can easily be moved wherever other family members are, indoors or outdoors
- the opportunity to see the patterns of day-to-day life and start to build up associations and make connections that aid brain development (for example, when the buggy comes out soon I'll be out in the fresh air, or when the front door opens daddy/big brother/big sister is coming home)
- exposure to the sounds of his native language(s) as others go about their day, or stop to chat to baby, or sing him a song
- practice building up the muscles in the back, neck, legs and arms while lying on his tummy and on his back, all of which are the foundation for fundamental skills such as holding his own head up, rolling over, sitting up, crawling and eventually walking
- the chance to explore his own hands and feet – at first babies do not realise that these are actually part of their own body but with freedom of movement they gradually become aware of this and begin to control the movements, reaching out to grab things and see what they do; at this stage a few rattles or early toys can be placed on the mat for your baby to explore.

Treasure baskets

Babies are natural explorers so a 'treasure basket' full of a wide variety of natural everyday objects made of different materials is an ideal way to spark their curiosity. Treasure baskets are ideal for babies who can sit comfortably but are not yet mobile. They help babies literally get 'in touch with their world' as they hold and explore (often also with their mouths) a range of objects. Find a basket with a broad base and flat sides, preferably with no handles to get in the way of reaching in. Choose objects from around your home that are small enough to be held but large enough not to be swallowed; look for objects that make a noise, and objects that can be sucked, held, banged, or rolled. The more objects the better, so that there is a choice and to stimulate curiosity and interest. If your baby is not interested remove the object and try something else – a treasure basket should be organic and evolve with your baby.

Here are some ideas for objects to put in a treasure basket:

- pine cones
- pebbles
- wooden nail brush
- feathers
- pumice stone
- small loofah
- small natural sponge
- lemon
- small egg whisk
- bunch of keys
- bells
- short lengths of chain
- leather purse
- small cloth bags of lavender or rosemary
- powder puff
- bath plug with chain
- small cardboard boxes
- tinfoil
- whatever you see around you that you think might interest your baby!

Treasure baskets

Most of the objects in Travis's basket have been collected around the house, or have been bought in kitchen, interior decorating and bathroom shops. I initially started with things that were soft and of varying textures to see what he would like. I put in some fruits, some metal and wooden objects, a small Clarins tester box, a small metal Earl Grey tin, an ice cream cup and many other items. Initially he loved the tester box and the ice cream cup. He turned them over and over to look at and feel. The metal items were also a hit, but surprisingly the soft toys and materials were not looked at for long. I therefore took out most of the soft toys, and replaced them with others of varying textures. I noticed that Travis did not show any interest in the blue wooden fish, so just to see what happened I changed it for an orange one and he loved it.

I began to watch with glee as he repeatedly played with certain objects, and avoided others. I was unsure as to whether he didn't like them or just didn't know what to do with them. I sat down with him and went through some of the objects that he showed less interest in... To my excitement some of the objects were greatly received thereafter...

As Travis got older I noticed that he now liked to bang things together, so I introduced a small metal pot and spoon, which were received with delight. His tambourine was bashed for hours, and he also loved to play with his decorative balls (bought from an interior design shop, they are used to display in bowls on your dining room table). They were marvellous as one was made out of porcelain, one woven out of twigs, another from seeds, a rough string one and another woven out of grass. The textures were amazing and he used to turn them over and over, looking at the different patterns and designs. ...The Treasure Baskets are now in demand from all my friends...They have seen the way Travis plays for long periods of time, gently talking/singing to himself, completely enraptured and content with what he is doing.

Louise Lord, first published in *Montessori International* (2006)

It is very important that your baby can select and choose the objects that are of interest to her. Look around your home and use your imagination; think about stimulating all the senses – touch (including texture, shape and weight), smell, taste, sound and sight. Allow plenty of time for your baby to explore the basket, at least half an hour, when your baby is alert, refreshed and calm. You could use cushions to support your baby if needed. Ideally the treasure basket could become part of your daily routine.

Treasure baskets work so well because your baby takes the lead, so the experience is naturally stimulating without being over stimulating. Your baby controls how much time she wants to spend exploring the objects and to return to favourite things. The treasure basket promotes concentration and can lead to periods of complete absorption, sometimes up to an hour! Use this time as an opportunity to sit alongside your baby to observe and encourage your baby to explore without intervening: you do not need to handle the objects with your baby; let your baby explore independently.

Heuristic play

Once your baby becomes more mobile - crawling or walking - he will no longer be content to just feel objects; he will start to want to explore what he can actually do with objects, moving from thinking 'what is it?' to 'what can I do with it?'. This is the time to introduce heuristic play which is slightly different to the treasure basket, as this time you are using collections of lots of the same objects combined with different kinds of containers. This combination will provide your baby or toddler with opportunities to explore different ways of using, connecting, moving and transporting different objects. As with the treasure basket you do not need to spend any money; everything you need can be found around your home.

What kind of objects?

- wooden rings
- buttons
- ribbons
- corks
- bangles

- shells
- pegs
- pom poms
- lolly sticks
- keys

See what you can find around your home. You can store the objects in simple drawstring bags.

What kind of containers?

- paper carrier bags
- ice cube trays
- metals tins with lids
- cardboard tubes of any size
- big and small boxes
- paper cups
- egg cups
- kitchen roll holders (great for slotting on bangles or wooden curtain rings)

Again let your imagination be your guide as you search.

Set the objects out in a clearly defined space. Allow plenty of time for your child to play, up to an hour including time to tidy up. Put out some of the containers and some of the collections of objects for your child to explore. You can change the combinations on different days. Now sit back and watch! You will see your child transfer objects, move them around, arrange them, line them up, group objects, put objects in and take objects out of containers, push, pull and roll objects, bang objects together, pile and balance objects and knock them down again!

So, what is your child learning?

This form of play is helping your child explore the effects of his actions on objects. It allows him to find possibilities and patterns. It's about starting to form ideas, before language emerges, so your child will be learning fundamental notions such as 'round things roll', 'flat things can be piled up', or 'small things fit inside big things'.

Many commercial or manufactured toys designed for this age group are limited in their 'potential for discovery', having just one way that they can be used; they can also simply be too complicated. Heuristic play is open-ended and provides limitless opportunities that encourage experimentation, problem solving and trial-and-error learning.

Emerging play: the mobile explorer

As the baby becomes a toddler the mat or blanket gives way to an increasingly mobile explorer who will flourish given the freedom to move freely within both the indoor and outdoor space. As you continue to observe your child at play, you will see her grow and change, and by responding to these changes, you can encourage her growing independence as well as her development in all areas.

" As you continue to observe your child at play, you will see her grow and change, and by responding to these changes, you can encourage her growing independence as well as her development in all areas."

At this age, the child is becoming more and more independent and often enjoys joining in with daily life activities such as

- cooking
- laying the table
- sweeping
- mopping
- cleaning windows
- doing laundry
- washing the car
- gardening

Encourage this by giving the child his own 'tools' to use (his own rag and spray bottle full of water for cleaning, a child-size broom, dustpan and brush, real child-size garden tools). Allow your child to really get involved – the results won't be perfect and it will almost certainly take much longer than if you'd done it by yourself, but in the end it will be worth it when your child begins to master these basic life skills and can do them increasingly independently. Children's self-esteem will grow as they genuinely contribute to the upkeep and smooth running of their house and garden, and there will be more hands on deck for household tasks; it's a win-win situation.

Think about accessibility – can the child reach what they need? Space considerations may well mean that some things will need to be kept on higher shelves, but try to place as much as you can on low shelves so that the child does not need to ask for help from an adult to get things down as this interrupts her 'flow' of activity and stops her being independent in the space. If child-accessible space is an issue one option is to rotate toys and activities, keeping some on display and others in storage and periodically swapping them over.

> Allow your child to really get involved – the results won't be perfect and it will almost certainly take much longer than if you'd done it by yourself, but in the end it will be worth it when your child begins to master these basic life skills and can do them increasingly independently."

In order to create a space that is manageable for the child, try to minimise clutter so that the child can easily see what is available. Place toys in baskets on shelves, with all pieces to a set (farm animals, cars, a jigsaw) in the same container, rather than putting lots of toys jumbled together in a big toy box. This way there is no frustration over missing pieces, and no time wasted searching for what they want. Also, if children can see where things go, and reach the shelves on their own, it is much easier for them to tidy up themselves and make it ready for next time.

As for the toys themselves, there is still no need to spend a lot of money. As with the treasure baskets and collections for heuristic play for younger babies and toddlers, natural materials will appeal to the child, but there is nothing necessarily wrong with plastic toys; not a day goes by without our Duplo or Lego being played with, and our 'small world' toys have also been invaluable. Think about using natural objects such as shells, stones, sticks, leaves, conkers that you can collect with your child. These can be counted, sorted, matched; they can go in the tea set or play kitchen, be pushed around in a dumper truck, or be buried in the sand pit as 'treasure'. Keep it simple and look out for things that can be used in different ways such as wooden blocks – let your child's imagination be the focus, not the toy.

Within the play space, consider getting a child-size table with chairs for puzzles, games and other small activities such as setting up a farm. You might also consider getting a few throw rugs or mats for your child

to set out on the floor when she gets something out to play with. This clearly sets out her space and allows her the freedom to play however she would like within that space; this can be especially useful when you have more than one child, so each child can clearly see where the other child is playing and what they are using, and be encouraged to respect that space.

Arts and crafts

At this age the child will begin making things so consider setting up an art area. Look for a space near a sink, with an easy-to-clean floor or a sturdy plastic mat on the floor to wipe clean. A corner of the kitchen is often ideal but obviously you will need to use the space you have; it may make more sense to convert a small area of the utility room, or your child's bedroom. The key, as with the child's toys, is to make the materials as accessible to your child as possible so that he is free to create whatever he wants, whenever he wants, without asking for an adult to get things out for him.

Materials for a first art area might include:
- playdough and cutters
- a selection of different types of paper
- markers, crayons and pencils (plus a sharpener and rubber)
- paints and large brushes
- craft materials (gather bits and bobs such as milk bottle tops, toilet rolls, bits of ribbon or string, odd pieces of fabric, ice lolly sticks)
- real scissors not plastic – plastic scissors can be frustrating because they don't actually cut very well; instead show the child how to carry and use metal scissors made for children with rounded edges
- tape and glue
- an easel, if there is space for one
- somewhere to dry things
- an area for display (using magnets on the fridge, of course, but also consider a notice board, portfolio, display mounts or other ways of sharing your child's creations – mine sometimes enjoy sending their creations to family and friends but other times they are keen to keep them)

As the child gets older consider adding different materials to the art area

to keep it alive and interesting. As fine motor skills develop the child will be able to manipulate smaller paint brushes and finer felt tip markers to create more detailed artwork. Consider showing the child (or learning together) how to do simple knitting, woodworking, or modelling with clay, for example.

Sharing stories

Babies and toddlers also love books, stories, rhymes and songs. Singing and nursery rhymes carry on from baby's first days, and the bedtime story is a nice way to wind down the day, but there are many other opportunities for fitting these in through the day as well. Consider listening to music or stories in the car, or while doing other things such as cooking or cleaning. Babies can have their own library cards and the library is a fantastic resource for all sorts of books as well as stories on tape/CD. Keep baskets of books in different rooms in the house, perhaps next to the sofa or armchair, on the toy shelf, or in the bedroom; baskets can be easily moved where they are needed – out into the garden on a sunny day, say, or with you in the car on a long journey – and let the child look at the fronts of the books rather than just the spine when choosing what she would like to read. If you have a book on a theme consider whether it might go in the basket with those toys, so a board book about 'things that go' in the cars tub, or a touch-and-feel book about farm animals in with the farm toys.

Bedtime stories

Reading with my daughter at bedtime is something that I absolutely treasure. It is a chance for just the two of us to enter into a shared world, and have a moment of uninterrupted connection. For me, the differences between reading bedtime stories and playing games with Mia are down to a couple of things – where we are and what I am thinking about. Being in the bedroom with the nightlight or a lamp on, and Mia wearing her pyjamas and holding her cup of milk, makes for a calm time that complements the excitement and joy we get from books. It helps me too – I can forget about what has gone on during the day, leave work worries behind, not be reminded of jobs around the house that need doing – the only thing I think about is my daughter and the books we share.

It doesn't always go smoothly though, at least from my adult point of view. Mia will sometimes insist on choosing seven or eight books to read, on occasion she will close every story half way through and every now and then will turn pages back and forth just so they are repeated again and again. But if Montessori has taught me anything, it is the value of 'following the child'. I remember that what we are doing is not just about reading a story from start to finish. Mia is taking the lead by choosing which books to read and she is definitely in control of how they are read. I know it is good for her to hear me tell stories, to hear the tone and rhythm in my voice. And more than all that we are spending time together on her terms without distraction or disturbance – if we can finish story time with a hug and a kiss as she settles down to sleep then I know I must be doing something right.

Jeremy, Montessori teacher and father of two, ages 2 and 8

Organising a play space as your child grows

As children grow play changes. By understanding this and observing how they play you can continue to help them get the most out of their play.

- As children reach age three to four, their play becomes more social, and they begin playing with other children rather than just alongside them. Children of this age talk in complete sentences and have an ever-growing vocabulary, which allows them to increasingly use language to initiate play sequences, interact with others and take their play to a new level.
- Then around age four to five, play becomes more creative and collaborative and involves developing more detailed 'storylines', such as cushions as stepping stones across crocodile-infested waters.
- By around age six, children tend to organise their own play in the

> Play comes from the child's imagination not the toy, so expensive toys are not necessary to create fun and meaningful play. Look out for open-ended toys or 'found' objects."

environment that surrounds them, beginning with their own idea and
making it happen.

At all these stages the key ideas continue to be freedom in the space
(indoors and out), and access to what they need.

Play comes from the child's imagination not the toy, so expensive toys
are not necessary to create fun and meaningful play. Look out for open-
ended toys or 'found' objects such as pieces of fabric, dressing up hats and
bags, and building blocks. These things are often readily accessible and
need not be expensive. These simple things encourage creativity and
problem-solving by being able to use the same object in different ways.
For example a paper plate can be a steering wheel, a spaceship, or a face
(of a person, or an animal, or a monster, or an alien, or...), and an empty
box (the bigger the better, in our house!) can be a house, a castle, a
rocket, a train, a cage, a robot, a ship; the possibilities are endless. If you
are handy with tools, you and your child could even saw and sand pieces
of log to make your own open-ended building materials.

At play on holiday

Observing my three children at play when we are on holiday, without all the toys that fill the shelves at home, is an interesting experience. Free to use indoor and outdoor space and a selection of everyday household objects, their play really blossoms. I might observe:

■ lots of sand and water play (at the beach, or in the bathtub or kitchen sink), pouring, mixing, building, scooping, filling and emptying with different sized scoops, tubs, cups, bottles and funnels.

What are these children learning?

They are experimenting with quantities, measuring, textures, and the properties of different materials (wet sand vs dry sand), while practicing fine motor skills. They are also often co-operating and discussing what they are doing.

■ building a den with sofa cushions and blankets, or using sofa cushions to create an obstacle course

What are these children learning?

They are learning to work together to create something, practicing gross motor skills such as climbing, jumping and crawling, and experimenting with basic principles of construction.

■ a role play that might include dressing up using different hats, bags and pieces of fabric (for example scarves, or old sheets) that could be a cape, or a Roman toga, or a market stall awning, or a wedding dress, or...

What are these children learning?

They are engaging in creative, imaginative play, working together to develop a story or theme, using language skills to narrate the story, create dialogue, negotiate roles and so on. In adapting the fabric to their needs, they are using problem-solving skills in a creative way.

Reading and writing with your child

It is a natural desire to want your child to learn to read and write because these skills form the foundation of so much later learning. However it is important to keep in mind that children will all learn at a different pace and hit their sensitive periods for learning different things at different times. The key in the early years is building a foundation by creating an atmosphere where books are used and enjoyed, and where the child learns to love books and storytelling. If children have been read to and love books and stories they will learn to read in their own time, when they are ready.

As for writing, Montessori believed that writing naturally came before reading. Let children see writing in real life practical contexts (shopping lists, thank you notes, invitations, emails), and provide stationery and good pencils for them to use to do their own writing when they are ready. But try not to push pencil work too soon; instead encourage activities that build strength in the small muscles of the hand and the use of a pincer grip (using the same muscles we use to hold a pencil).

Examples include:

- painting with big brushes
- playing with Lego
- doing knobbed puzzles
- pouring drinks and serving food
- opening and closing (small bottles, padlocks, jars)
- doing up zips, buttons, clips and other fastenings

Thinking about maths

There is no need to 'do maths' with the young child. Counting,
numbers, shapes and sizes, measuring, sorting, pairing and matching;
these are all part of the child's world:

- Stories, rhymes, and songs often include counting and other maths skills such as shapes and sizes.

- Board games, cards, and dice games are excellent for practicing maths skills from simple number recognition and counting up to complicated operations such as multiplication and division.

- Cooking involves measuring and estimating skills.

- Sorting, pairing and matching by size and shape is the basis for many children's games (such as memory and lotto games) and puzzles, but it also takes place in all sorts of everyday contexts – gathering the right blocks to build something, pairing shoes or matching socks, or comparing different tomatoes grown in the garden for example.

- Dealing with money is great for skills such as addition, subtraction, rounding and counting by twos, fives and tens.

- Activities such as setting the table or handing out treats to friends is a natural way to practice one-to-one correspondence.

- Cutting cakes, pizzas or playdough equally is early fractions work.

Baking muffins: maths in the kitchen

1. Paul counts out 3 eggs and breaks them into the bowl, before carefully pouring on the milk, stopping when he gets to 100ml.

2. Paul mixes the eggs and milk with the electric whisk. He is proud of doing it by himself.

3. Paul carefully spoons the flour onto the scales; he concentrates and stops when he gets to 300 grams.

A Montessori-inspired kitchen

Infants and toddlers

From around six months of age babies will be ready to try solid foods. As with other sensitive periods, there is no fixed timetable, but by observing carefully you should be able to tell when they are ready. Signs might include any of the following, but keep in mind that many babies will start to demonstrate some of these around three to four months of age but will not necessarily be ready to try solids until closer to six months:

- increased curiosity about mealtimes and food generally
- being consistently unsatisfied with usual milk feeds
- fascination with watching others eat, following fork to mouth and back again
- trying to grab food from you
- mimicking chewing as you eat

Child-led weaning is an approach that means letting your child take the lead in feeding himself and letting him explore a range of finger

4. Paul adds spices and raisins, making decisions about how much to put in. He is using his senses of smell and taste to guide him.	5. Paul mixes the ingredients and then spoons the mixture into the muffin pan, one spoon for each hole. He counts as he spoons in the mixture.	6. Paul waits 15 minutes until the muffins are ready; he sees the steam rising out of the hot muffins and lets them cool before putting them on the plate.

foods and different types of food, moving on to food the rest of the family is eating, perhaps mashed with the back of a fork rather than pureed.

As your baby becomes a toddler think about how you could make the things she needs to use in the kitchen more accessible, to encourage independence:

- If possible, put the child's plates, cups and cutlery in a low cupboard or on a low shelf so she can get what she needs herself.
- Look at whether easy-to-access snacks such as breadsticks, boxes of raisins, fruit, or small yogurts could be placed within the child's reach, on the bottom shelf in the pantry and/or on a specific shelf in the fridge.
- Encourage your child to choose his own snack at a time when he is ready for it.
- Set up a place where your toddler can pour her own drink, and show her what to do when there are spills.

Toddlers love to be involved, so create a space where they can help out with whatever is happening in the kitchen (this may be as simple as pushing a chair up to the counter for them to stand on, or setting aside a workspace at a child-size table in the kitchen). Give them real tasks to do, such as greasing a tin or pouring ingredients into a cake mix, and resist the urge to interfere as they do them. There will inevitably be mess, so be ready to show them how to clean up any spills so that they can start doing this on their own as well.

Older children

As children get older they are soon ready for more independence and more responsibility in the kitchen. Some ideas to think about:

- Consider moving from plastic to ceramic plates and metal cutlery as early as possible, so that the child has a reason to take responsibility for carrying dishes properly. This can be tricky if for example you have younger children as well; our five-year-old currently can't reach the cupboard with the plates and glasses he uses because our two-year-old isn't ready for carrying them across our tiled kitchen floor. When she is, we'll move them to a lower cupboard but in the meantime he has to ask for help to get them.

Montessori around the house

When I had my children I dreamt of low shelves in the kitchen, child-sized sinks in the bathroom and all that. Seven years on I haven't changed anything. Both my sons love helping out with the housework and cooking. They know of the dangers such as hot ovens or sharp knives but they have themselves found a way to get around our environment by using stools and other props in order to carry out any task.

Chopping vegetables, peeling onions, rolling out dough are activities that we do together while we chat about our day in school. They also love baking and then we measure quantities, use the scales, count spoonfuls of sugar...lots to learn there!

Lately they are going through a sensitive period for polishing their school shoes, so we have set up a box for them with a cloth, brush and some neutral polish. I explained to them about using some newspaper to cover the floor and how to spread a bit of polish first then brush gently until the shoes get shiny. I hope this one lasts for a few years!

Amalia, Montessori teacher and mother of two, ages 3 and 7

- Demonstrate how to use a knife, starting off with cutting soft things like bananas and spreading things on toast or crackers. Then once the child is comfortable with this demonstrate how to handle, carry and use a sharp knife to chop things with. Although at first this may feel more dangerous, if the child knows how something works and how to use it safely they are ultimately far safer than a child who has never been allowed to hold an object happening across one and starting to experiment.

- Encourage your children to help themselves to breakfast, drinks and snacks. Again, look at whether what they need is accessible; if they can make toast but can't reach the toaster to get started perhaps a re-jig of the kitchen layout would help.

From the early days the importance of shared mealtimes can't be overstated. This time is a learning experience on so many levels:

- Shared mealtimes are a real-life opportunity to learn about and practice table manners; remember that you will need to explain how and why things are done as they are (often many times!) and also demonstrate what you expect.

- A shared meal offers an opportunity to connect as a family and share what is happening for each person.
- Serving meals 'family style' where each person serves themselves (rather than plating up and serving everyone a full plate) allows freedom of choice and independence, respecting that not everyone likes the same things or in the same way.
- It can be tricky to cook for a family: try to encourage variety in what is on offer, but at the same time respect that everyone will have their own likes and dislikes; one possibility is to have each family member choose one meal a week, and reserve one meal for a family favourite, or trying something new.
- Involve even the youngest children at all stages in the process, from menu planning and grocery shopping to cooking, laying the table and serving the meal, to cleaning up afterwards.

A Montessori-inspired bathroom

Considering freedom of movement and independence, have a look at the bathroom in your home from your child's height and consider what she needs to be able to "do it herself" in this room:

- a sturdy step stool that ideally enables her to reach the taps (not just the basin)
- a low hook for hanging up her towel
- her own shelf in the bath or shower for things like toiletries, flannel or bath toys

As children get older they will naturally take on increasing independence to manage their own routines of having a shower or bath, brushing teeth and so on.

You may feel you want your child to potty train as early as possible, but children can be ready to tackle this at widely differing ages, from just before two to around three and a half. As so many of us have learned, if they aren't ready they just aren't ready! Embarking on toilet training when your child shows they are ready (so in a 'sensitive period' for learning this key skill) will make this task a much quicker and easier one for all concerned, with fewer accidents.

A Montessori-inspired garden/outdoor space

As we have seen, Montessori placed a lot of importance on allowing the child free movement between indoor and outdoor space, and on encouraging children to explore the natural world around them in detail. Where you live will obviously dictate what the surrounding 'natural world' means to your family. This is perfectly fine; it isn't necessary to live in a rural setting with an enormous back garden to appreciate the natural world!

Gardening

Most children will love digging in the dirt; it's a small step then to add some seeds and water and you are away with gardening. If you live in a flat, you might grow herbs, flowers and vegetables in window boxes, and also let children look after house plants. If you have an outdoor space of your own, consider giving children their own space to look after, which could be a corner of the garden itself, or a few tubs or

pots. Give them real child-size tools, not plastic copies (these are often toys that are not actually fit for purpose, which leads to frustration) and let them start by digging to explore what the soil is like. As with knives in the kitchen and scissors in the art area, show them how to use real tools safely rather than keeping them out of reach. Move on to planting seeds; cress is an obvious place to start because it germinates quickly, but let them choose things they like to eat if possible (sadly my three all love watermelon which is hopeless in our climate). Make sure they have their own watering can in a manageable size, and explain what plants need to grow, then let them watch the results. Expand vocabulary by using proper names for everything.

Pets

Keeping a pet can be a wonderful learning experience for a child. A pet shows the child first-hand what animals are like and offers an easy point of comparison for the rest of the animal kingdom. Looking after a pet teaches responsibility. Pets can also be early friends and teach a child valuable lessons about how to respect others because it is straight-forward to see the impact your behaviour has on the animal; if you are gentle with our new kittens, they purr and roll over to be stroked, but if you are rough with them, they run away, or try to scratch or bite you to show they don't like it. Pets can also be an introduction to the idea that every life has a beginning, middle and an end.

Out and about

Even if you do not have a lot of outdoor space at home, there are always opportunities to get outdoors and experience nature. Some ideas to try, in the city or in the country:

- take your child out animal tracking, looking for signs of different animals, insects and birds that live in your local area

- make up your own nature "treasure" hunts; this ties in nicely with young children's love of small objects and attention to detail

- find a bag and go on a collecting hunt; bring back whatever natural objects your child notices (within reason!) and let them choose what to do with them once they are home – they may choose to make a collage, or set up a miniature nature museum, or build an obstacle course for their hamster; the possibilities truly are endless!

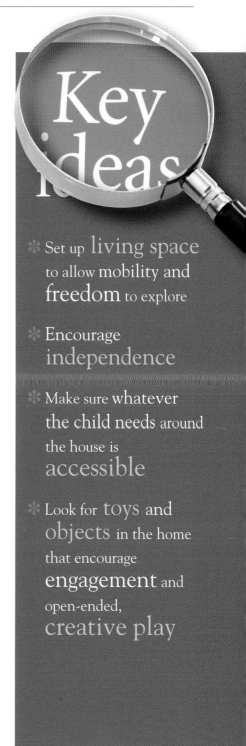

Key ideas

* Set up living space to allow mobility and freedom to explore

* Encourage independence

* Make sure whatever the child needs around the house is accessible

* Look for toys and objects in the home that encourage engagement and open-ended, creative play

My relationship with Ophir, like all relationships, is about acceptance and trust. In each moment I am challenged by my own prejudices and fears. To witness a child - with disabilities or not - grow up and allow them to develop as themselves, to nurture potential but not overwhelm is a daunting task facing all parents. With a child who has a disability it is hard to ignore the task. Even the most mundane experiences are heightened and intensified. The pace of life is slowed down and so these feelings that accompany this journey unavoidably rise to the surface daily.

My struggle has been to stay close enough to a core sense of myself and not to be seduced by an external image of "how to live" and "what's important" but to a vision created by just us in the present reality of our lives. When you have a learning difficulty you already live outside a well-defined box. Often being "different" can be liberating.

Fiona, mother of two, aged 9 and 16

First published in *Up Close: A Mother's View*, by **Fiona Yaron-Field**

In conclusion

Hopefully you have found *Learning Together* to be a useful and enjoyable read. I hope that you may be inspired to try out some of the ideas, adapting them to best meet the needs of your family. Above all, I hope that Montessori's vision of following the child has been brought home to you and that you enjoy following your children on their path, wherever it may lead.

If you're interested in finding out more about Montessori and her approach:

- *What You Should Know About Your Child*, by Maria Montessori, (1989) Oxford: ABC Clio

- *Montessori Today*, by Paula Polk Lillard, (1996) New York: Schocken

- *Montessori from the Start*, by Paula Polk Lillard and Lynn Lillard Jensen, (2003) New York: Schocken

- *Montessori International* magazine, published by Montessori Centre International www.montessorimagazine.org.uk

- *How to Raise an Amazing Child: The Montessori Way*, by Tim Seldin (2006) New York: Dorling Kindersley

If you'd like to learn more on different areas of child development:

- *Why Love Matters: How Affection Shapes a Baby's Brain* by Sue Gerhardt, (2004) Oxford: Routledge

- *The Well-balanced Child*, by Sally Goddard-Blythe, (2005) Stroud: Hawthorn Press

- *How Babies Think*, by Alison Gopnik, Patricia Kuhl and Andrew Meltzoff, (1999) London: Weidenfeld & Nicolson

- *Everything your Baby Would Ask ... If Only He or She Could Talk*, by Annette Kamiloff-Smith and Kyra Kamiloff, (2003) London: Carrol & Brown

- *What Mothers Do: Especially When it Looks Like Nothing*, by Naomi Stadlen, (2004) London: Piaktus

If you want to know more about parenting and promoting positive behaviour through respectful interactions:

- *The Complete Secrets of Happy Children*, by Steve Biddulph, (2003) London: Thorsons

- *How to Talk So Kids Will Listen and Listen So Kids Will Talk* by Adele Faber & Elaine Mazlish, (2001) London: Piccadilly Press

- *Nonviolent Communication: A Language of Life*, by Marshall Rosenberg, (2003) Encinitas CA: Puddledancer Press

Useful organisations

Adoption UK offers support on all aspects of adoptive parenting
www.adoptionuk.org

Gingerbread provides advice and support for single parents
www.gingerbread.org.uk

Family and Parenting Institute has a section for parents with information about how you can help your child learn through play
www.earlyhomelearning.org.uk
You can also download a range of publications
www.familyandparenting.org

Families in the Foundation Years has a comprehensive section of information on all aspects of parenting
www.foundationyears.org.uk/parents

Fatherhood Institute has an information service which provides advice and support for fathers including activities for dads
www.fatherhoodinstitute.org

National Literacy Trust provides advice for developing language through books, songs and rhymes
www.wordsforlife.org.uk
and resources to download
www.literacytrust.org.uk/talktoyourbaby

ICAN provides information to parents about speech, language and communication
www.ican.org.uk

Parentline Plus has a 24 hour helpline 0808 800 2222 or visit
www.parentlineplus.org.uk

Parenting UK aims to raise awareness about parenting issues through a parent portal with links to resources and parent courses
www.parentinguk.org

If you'd like to follow Montessori parenting blogs:

www.howwemontessori.typepad.com

www.sewliberated.typepad.com

www.montessorihomes.blogspot.com

 /montessoriUK

 @montessoriUK

 /montessoriORG

blog.montessori.org.uk

If you have enjoyed this book and would like to know more about **Montessori** order your FREE **Discovering Montessori DVD**:
dvd@montessori.org.uk

Designed and produced in the UK by Stuart O'Neil, Design for Print (UL) Limited
Printed by Abbey Printers, Newton Abbot

M ∘ E ∘ A ∘ B

If you want to know more about finding a Montessori school:

- Visit our website www.montessori.org.uk and follow the links to find a school.

- The Montessori Evaluation and Accreditation Board was established in January 2008 to ensure that all schools using the Montessori name in the UK offer high-quality Montessori education and care.

- We only accredit schools that demonstrate genuine Montessori practice and are committed to continuing development. There are currently over 100 accredited schools.

- You can check which schools are accredited and read the accreditation reports by visiting the MEAB website: montessori.org.uk/msa/accreditation

MONTESSORI
CENTRE INTERNATIONAL

If you want to know more about training to be a Montessori teacher:

- Visit our website www.montessori.org.uk/mci_training
  We are Europe's largest training college.

- We offer courses in London and accredited centres across the UK and overseas.

- In partnership with London Metropolitan University, we offer a full and part-time Foundation Degree (Montessori Early Childhood Practice) course.

- A part-time and distance learning International Diploma course in Montessori pedagogy is also available.

- Regular open evenings are held. Details of these and our courses can be found on the website.

- To make an appointment for an interview, email: admissions@montessori.org.uk